How to Pray

A step by step guide on how to pray correctly

Voice of Islam VOI TELEVISION

ANOTHER VOICE OF ISLAM COMMUNITY PROJECT

Bringing the message of Islam to all people

www.voitv.org

First published in November 2010 by:
Voice of Islam Trust
Reprinted 2020

Booklet published and distributed by:

Voice of Islam Trust
PO Box 97 920
Manukau 2241
Auckland, New Zealand
Email: info@voitv.org
www.voitv.org

Voice of Islam Ghana
PO Box CO 3163
TEMA
Ghana
Email: info@voitv.org
www.voitv.org

Printed in India by Goodword Books
info@goodwordbooks.com

ISBN: 978-0-473-17721-8 (set)

Voice of Islam VOI TELEVISION

Preface

In the name of Allah the Beneficent the Merciful.

All praise is due to Allah, and may the peace and blessings be upon His final messenger Muhammad and upon those who follow in his footsteps until the last day.

The main purpose of this booklet is to help new Muslims learn how to perform the prayer (the second pillar of Islam) properly and as quickly as possible.

Although not intended as a comprehensive book of prayer it is a good beginner's guide to the correct manner to perform prayer in Islam.

We do suggest that you do not use this kit on its own, you should get a friend or colleague to help you in your prayer this will enable you to grasp the techniques much sooner... God Willing.

It is compulsory that the prayer is recited in Arabic (the English translation provided within is for your understanding of the Arabic and should not be uttered during prayer). It is very important that the correct pronunciation of the Arabic is learnt from the beginning as it can be difficult to relearn it later.

Do not worry if you find the pronunciation of the transliterated Arabic difficult at first, it takes practice and God willing you will eventually learnt it. As Muslims we have to always strive to do the best we can and in prayer we should always strive to perfect it for Gods pleasure.

As this booklet is only a simple introductive guide we suggest for comprehensive details on prayer that you should read specialized and detailed books on this subject.

Once you are confident in the correct performance of your prayer and do not need this prayer kit we ask that you please pass it on to others who can make good use of it.

Performing your prayers correctly and in there prescribed

times gains you the pleasure of Allah and thus fulfilling a very important and rewarding part of your deen (way of life).

Successful are indeed the believers, those who are humble in their prayer…

Qur'an: Al-Mu'minun 23 Ayah 1-2.

This success promised for our prayer can only be gained when we observe our prayers perfectly and in their fixed times.

Chairman
Voice of Islam Trust

Introduction

Before you begin

Before you begin the prayer there are certain requirements that have to be fulfilled and in the correct order otherwise the prayer will be invalid and not accepted by Allah.

These requirements are:

1. The time of prayer must have commenced.
2. The intention to pray - Niyah.
3. Purification and cleanliness - Taharah.
4. Ablution - Wudu.
5. Facing the direction of the Kabah (in Mecca, Saudi Arabia). This is known as the Qiblah.
6. Place of prayer (Salah)
7. Dress for prayer (Salah)
8. Types of prayer (Salah)
9. Number of Units (rakat) for the five compulsory prayers
10. Missed prayers (Salah)

1. The Prayers (Salah)

Definition: The Arabic word for the five compulsory prayers and other legislated prayers is Salah.

Prayer constitutes one pillar of Islam and is considered the foundation of our religion. It should be borne in mind that Allah does not need our prayer, because He is free of all needs. Allah is only interested in our prosperity and well being in every sense. When Allah emphasises the necessity of prayer or charges us with any duty, He means to help us; because whatever good we do is for our own benefit, and whatever offence we commit is against our own souls. The benefit which people can derive from Islamic prayer is immeasurable, and the blessing of prayer is beyond imagination. This is not just a theory or an assumption, it is a fact borne out by spiritual experience.

When we analyse the unique nature of the Islamic prayer we see that it is not merely a physical motion or a void recital of the Holy Book. It is a matchless unprecedented formula of intellectual meditations and spiritual devotion, of moral elevation and physical exercise. It is an exclusively Islamic experience where every muscle of the body joins the soul and the mind in the worship and glorification of Allah. It is difficult for anyone to impart in words the full meaning of the Islamic prayer, yet it can be said that it is:

- A lesson in discipline and willpower; as it is a training program designed to control evil desires and passions.
- A practice in devotion to Allah and all worthy objectives;
- A constant reminder of Allah's greatness and it brings men and women closer to Him;
- A seed that cultivates spiritual and moral soundness, as it purifies the heart, develops the mind and comforts the soul;
- A guide to the most upright way of life as it is the demonstration of our obedience to our Creator;
- A safeguard against indecency and evil, against deviation, shameful and forbidden activities;
- A demonstration of true equality, solid unity and fellowship;
- An expression of thankfulness to Allah and appreciation of Him;
- A cause of inner peace, stability and a means of cleanliness, purity and punctuality;
- An abundant source of patience, courage, hope and confidence.
- A fostering of the good and decent elements in us, and suppressing the evil and indecent inclinations.

This explains the Islamic prayer, and what it can do for us. The best testimony to this statement is to experience the prayer yourself and then you will know what it really means.

The Importance of the time for prayer

There is great importance placed on the times for prayer. We are told in the Qur'an and Hadith (the recorded sayings of Prophet Muhammad - peace be upon him) the time for these prayers and the great rewards we will receive by praying them in the correct time, and more importantly in the early stages of those times.

If we look at the five compulsory prayers and the time they are to be performed we see that there is merit in these times. As Muslims we are always taught that we should remember Allah and glorify Him much.

1. The dawn prayer (fajr) must be observed between dawn and sunrise (approximately 1 hour 40 minutes after the break of dawn). So the first thing we do to begin a new day is pray to Allah for His forgiveness and thank Him for bringing us into a new day.

Holy Qur'an: Hud (11) Ayah: 114

"Establish Salah (prayer) at the two ends of the day and in some watches of the night. Surely! Good deeds annul ill deeds. This is a reminder for the mindful."

2. The Noon Prayer (or midday prayer zuhr) is due when the sun begins its decline from its highest point at noon. During our busy day at work, study, or looking after the children at home we take time out from these worldly activities to remember our Creator and Sustainer.

Holy Qur'an: Al-Isra (17) Ayah: 78

"Perform your prayer from midday till the darkness of the night (i.e. the midday, mid afternoon, sunset and night prayers), and recite the Qur'an in the early dawn (the morning prayer). Verily, the recitation of the Qur'an in the early dawn is ever witnessed."

3. The Afternoon Prayer (asr) begins in the mid-afternoon (the middle time between the midday prayer and sunset). Here again we take time our to remember Allah.

Holy Qur'an: Al-Baqarah (2) Ayah: 238

"Guard strictly (the five compulsory) prayers especially the mid afternoon (i.e. the best prayer). And stand before Allah with obedience [and do not speak to others during the prayers]."

4. The Sunset Prayer (mughrib) is due after sunset. This usually falls after work, and we are thankful for the blessings that Allah has bestowed on us and our family.

Holy Qur'an: Hud (11) Ayah: 114

"Establish Salah (prayer) at the two ends of the day and in some watches of the night. Surely! Good deeds annul ill deeds. This is a reminder for the mindful."

5. The Night Prayer (isha) can be observed after the twilight disappears from the sky (approximately 1 hour 40 minutes past sunset). This is performed at the end of the day and is usually the last thing we do before we go to sleep. Thus we end the day as we begun it; remembering the One who allowed us to continue living in this world. So we should be thankful!

Holy Qur'an: An-Nur (24) Ayah: 58

"O you who believe! Let those among you who have not reached the age of puberty seek your permission (before they come to your bedroom) on three occasions: before the early morning prayer, while you have your midday rest, and after the late night prayer. These times are privacy for you..."

The Prophet (pbuh) said:

"Verily when a Muslim makes Wudu (ritual cleansing) properly and offers his Salah (prayer) with complete devotion and only for the sake of Allah his sins are shed away from him."

He also said:

"When a person offers his Salah (prayer) at its proper time with proper Wudu (ritual cleansing), with humility and submission and with all postures observed perfectly, then such a Salah rises up in a bright and beautiful form and blesses the person in these words; May Allah guard you as you have guarded me (i.e. the prayer [Salah]); On the other hand if a person is not punctual with his Salah, nor does he perform Wudu and postures of Salah perfectly or properly, then the Salah rises up in an ugly and dark shape and curses the person saying "May Allah ruin you as you have ruined me (Salah)" Then, it is flung back like a dirty rag at the face of the person."

May Allah save us all from this disgrace!

Holy Qur'an: Al-Kahf (18) Ayah: 28

"And keep your soul content with those who call on their Lord morning and evening, seeking His pleasure; and let not your eyes pass beyond them, seeking the pomp and glitter of this life; nor obey any whose heart We have permitted to neglect the remembrance of Us, one who follows his own desires, whose case has gone beyond all bounds."

Holy Qur'an: Al-Mu'minun (23) Ayah: 1-2

"Successful are indeed the believers, those who are humble in their Salah (prayer)."

This success is promised for our Salah can only be gained when we observe our Salah properly and perfectly and in there fixed times.

2. The Intention - Niyah

The Prophet (peace be upon him) said: "Actions are only by intention and every man has only that which he intended...!

The place of the intention is in the heart. Therefore it is not permissible to say the intention out loud or by the tongue as this was not the practice of the Prophet (peace be upon him).

3. Purification and cleanliness - Taharah

Cleanliness and hygiene are a very important aspect of a Muslim's life. It is not just a physical cleanliness but a spiritual one as well. So when it comes to preparing for prayer we have to ensure the clothing and place of prayer are clean and pure and free from impurities such as urine, faeces and any other impure substances.

Part of this cleanliness is that Muslims should always clean their private parts with water after going to the toilet as long is it does not cause injury (due to injury of sickness). If water is not available clean earth may be used as a substitute.

It is compulsory to have a shower (ghusl) after intimate relations between husband and wife, or after wet dreams and upon completion of a woman's monthly cycle (period) or postnatal bleeding.

Full shower or Ghusl is simple and requires the washing of your private parts with the left hand followed by washing the entire body starting from the right side.

4. Ablution - Wudu

Ablution maybe done with either clean fresh or salt water.

Before you commence the steps of Wudu you make your intention (in your heart) followed by Bismillah hir-rahma nir-raheem - in the name of Allah, most Gracious, most Merciful.

Actions for performing Wudu

Wash the hands up to the wrists (starting with the right hand) making sure that no part of the hands are left dry (3 times).

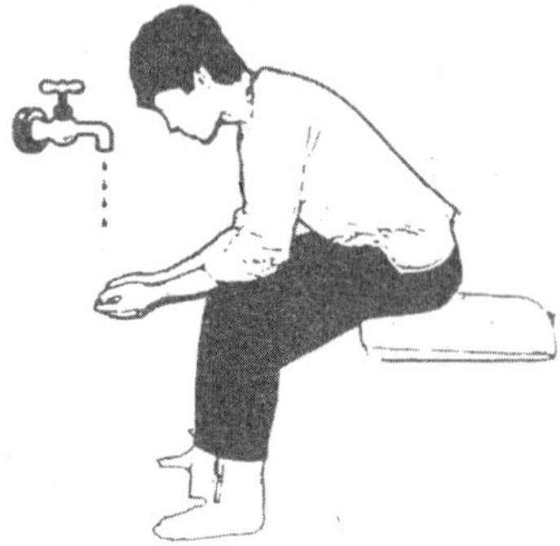

Rinse the mouth taking up water from right hand (3 times).

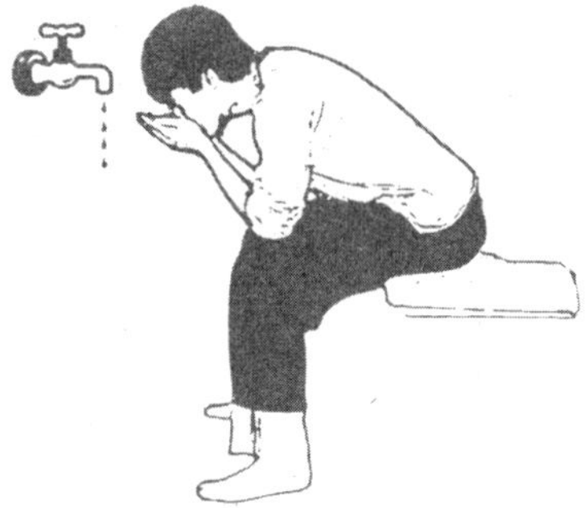

Clean the nose by sniffing water up up from the right palm and then eject water with the left hand (3 times).

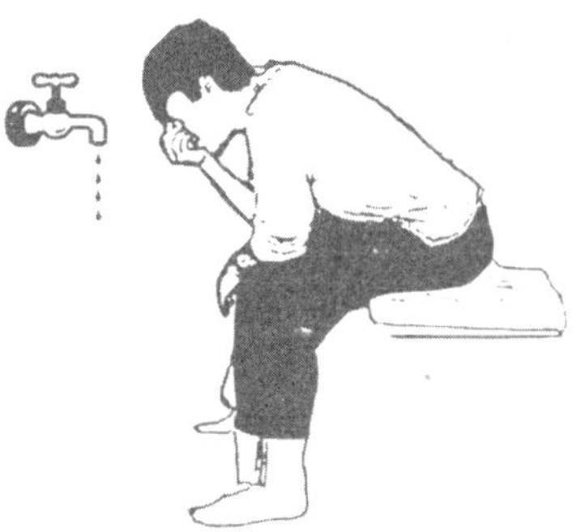

Wash the face, from ear to ear and forehead to chin making sure that no part of the face is left dry (3 times).

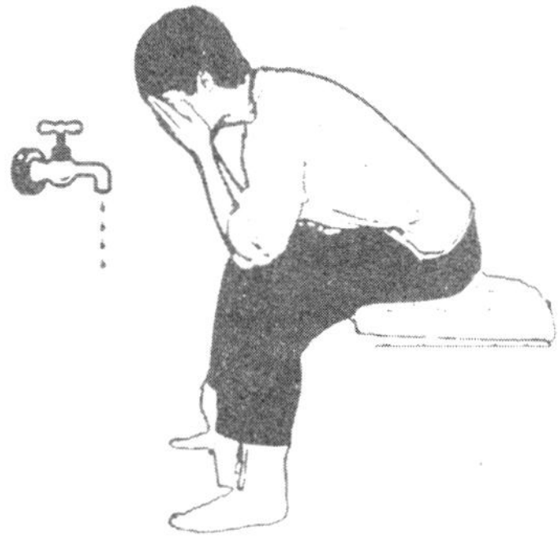

Then wash the forearms (starting with the right) up to the elbows making sure that no part is left dry (3 times).

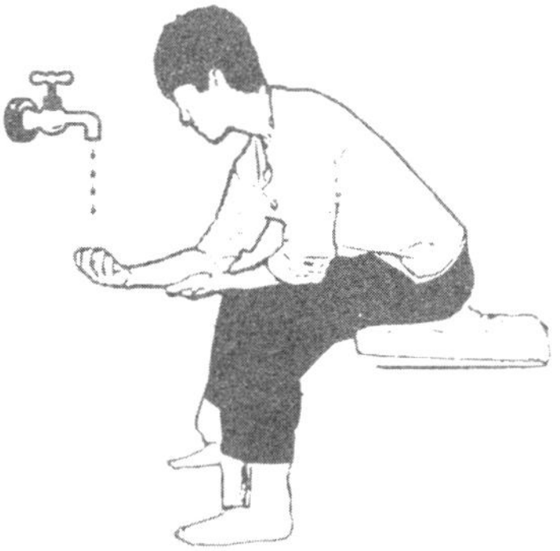

Rub the head as follows: Wet your finger and then wipe the head with your fingers, starting from the forehead, taking them to the nape of the neck, then bring them back to the forehead (once only)

Clean the ears by inserting the tips of the index fingers wet with water into the ears, twist them around the folds of the ears and at the same time pass the thumb behind the ears from the bottom, upwards (once only).

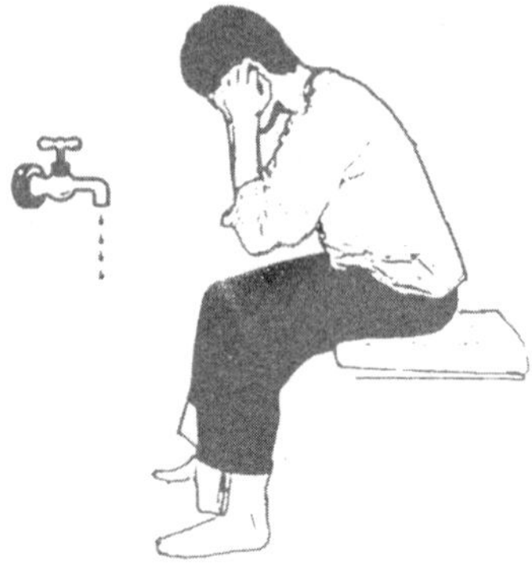

Wash the feet (right foot first) up to the ankles making sure that no parts of the feet are left dry, especially between the toes (3 times).

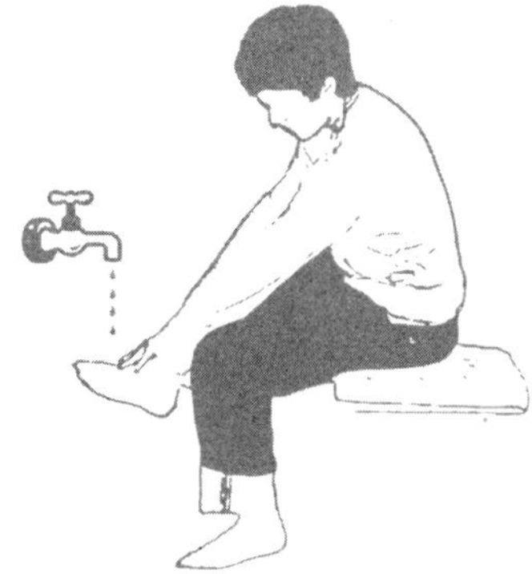

The Ablution (Wudu) is completed by saying the following supplication (Du'a):

Ash hadu an la ilaha illal lahu wah dahu la shareeka lahu wa ash hadu an-na Muhammadan abduhu wa rasuluhu.

Meaning: I testify there is no deity except Allah alone. And I testify that Muhammad is His servant and messenger.

What nullifies the Ablution (Wudu)

The following acts will cause your ablution to be broken and it will be necessary to redo it before you can perform your prayer.

- Going to the toilet
- Breaking wind
- Deep sleep
- Unconsciousness or intoxication
- Intimate relations between husband and wife
- Wet dreams

Note: A menstruating woman must not pray during this period and her missed prayers do not have to be made up.

5. Facing the direction of the Kabah in Makkah - The Qiblah.

Wherever a Muslim is in the world they must face towards the Kabah in Makkah for their prayer. There are special compasses designed to help you find the Qiblah location. If you have the Prayer Kit there is a compass included.

6. Place for prayer

A place or a building which is used for the purpose of prayer is called a Masjid (Mosque). A hadith tells us that "all the earth has been made for the Muslims, a mosque place for prayer (pure and clean)."

This means that wherever a Muslim might be they can offer their prayer but the reward for a prayer offered in a mosque is far greater than that offered in an ordinary place.

The following points should be noted when choosing a place for prayer.

- The place should be clean and pure. Prayer in a dirty, filthy and impure place such as a rubbish tip, slaughter house, toilet is forbidden.
- The place should be free from danger. The danger could be due to someone or something that may disturb the worshipper.

- You should not pray in a busy place that might disrupt others such as on the roads, footpath, the middle of a shopping centre etc.
- It is forbidden to pray on top or facing a grave.

7. Dress for prayer

Men:

- The clothing can be any style but should be loose fitting.
- The dress for men should be such that it covers from at least the naval to over the knees.
- It is also recommended to cover the shoulders.

Women:

- The clothing can be any style but should be loose and not transparent (they should not reveal the shape of the body).
- Only the face and the hands are permitted to be uncovered (so the feet should be covered).

8. Types of prayer

Compulsory (Fard) prayers

Fard prayers are compulsory and every believer is ordered by Allah to offer five compulsory prayers in each day. Failure to perform any one of the five compulsory prayers is a serious and punishable sin.

Optional (Sunnah) prayers

These are optional prayers which the Prophet (peace be upon him) performed before and after the compulsory prayer at special and isolated times. These also include prayers he encouraged the Muslims to pray.

This type of prayer can be broken into three types:

- Sunnah Mu'akkadah: These prayers are highly recommended by the Prophet (peace be upon him) and performed regularly by him before or after certain compulsory (fard) prayers.
- Sunnah: These prayers were offered occasionally by the

Prophet (peace be upon him)

- Extra (Nafl): This is an extra prayer which gains rewards for performing them but no sin if they are not performed. They can be performed by themselves according to the time and capacity of the believer. The Prophet (peace be upon him) encouraged the Muslim to pray the Nafl prayer to make up for any shortcomings in their Fard prayer.

9. Number of Units (rakat) for the five compulsory prayers

The following are the number of compulsory and optional units (rakat) associated with each prayer.

Prayer	Before Optional (sunnah)	**Compulsory (Fard)**	After Optional (sunnah)
Fajr (dawn)	2	**2***	
Zuhr (noon)	2 + 2	**4**	2 or (2 + 2)
Asr (mid afternoon)	2 + 2	**4**	
Maghrib (sunset)	2	**3***	2
Isha (night)	2	**4***	2 plus 3 witr

The Qur'anic recitation of the first two units (rakat) of each of the prayers that have an asterix (*) beside them must be recited aloud. All other units of these prayers should be recited silently.

The two units of optional (sunnah) prayers before the Fajr (dawn) and the two after the Maghrib (sunset) prayers are very important and should not be missed.

10. Missed Prayers

It is a major sin to miss a prayer deliberately; the missed prayer must be made up as soon as it is remembered. Any made up prayer is prayed in the same manner as it would have been done during its correct time.

Let's begin to pray

Intention - Niyah

After facing the Qiblah direction you should make an intention (niyah) within in your mind (silently). You should think about the particular prayer you are about to perform. You should not utter the words of intention (niyah) out loud, as this is not the approved practice of the Prophet (peace be upon him).

Performing one unit (rakat) of prayer

In the standing position, raise both hands to the shoulders with the palms facing out.

Then say the following:

Allahu Akbar
God is Great

Now place your hands on your chest, with the right hand placed over the left, and say the following:

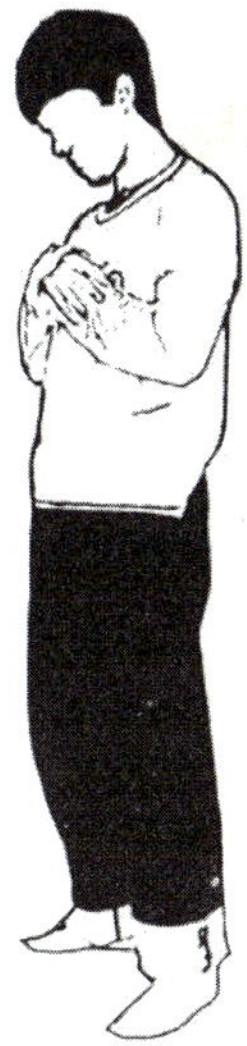

A'uthu billahi minash shayta nir-rajeem
I seek refuge with Allah from Satan the accursed

Then recite Surat-al Fatihah

Bismillah hir-rahma nir-raheem.
In the name of God, the Most Beneficent, the Most Merciful

Alhamdu lil-lahi rab-bil 'alameen.
Praise be to God the Lord of the Worlds

Ar rahma nir-raheem.
The Most Beneficent, the Most Merciful

Maliki yawmid - deen.
Master of the Day of Judgement

Iyyaka na'budu wa iyyaka nasta'een.
You alone we worship and in You alone we seek help

Ihdinas siratal mustakeem.
Guide us to the straight path

Siratal latheena an'amta alayhim.
The way of those whom You have favoured

Ghayril maghdoobi 'alayhim walad daa'leen.
Not the way of those who earned Your anger nor of those who have gone astray

****Ameen.***
Amen - Oh God answer our prayer!

* Although Ameen is pronounced during prayer it is not part of the Qur'an.

Next

Recite another chapter from the Qur'an if this is the 1st and 2nd unit (Rakat). We have inserted several more short chapters (Surahs) at the end of this booklet for your convenience.

There is no need to recite another chapter from the Qur'an if this is the 3rd and 4th unit.

Now recite Surah-ul Ikhlas

Bismillah hir-rahma nir-raheem.
In the name of God, the Most Beneficent, the Most Merciful

Qul huwal lahu ahad.
Say: "He is God, [who is] One,

Allah hus-samad.
God, the Eternal Refuge [the one sought in times of need and difficulty],

Lam yalid walam yulad.
He neither begets nor is born,

Walam yakul-lahu kufuwan ahad."
Nor is there to Him any equivalent."

Next

Raise both hands to the shoulders with the palms facing out.

Then say the following:

Allahu Akbar
God is Great

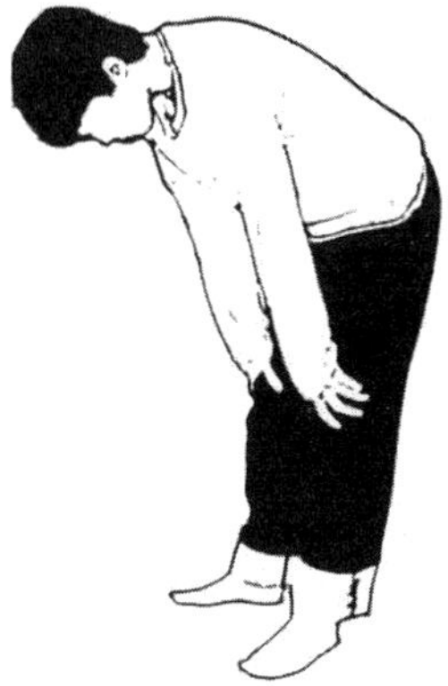

Now take up the bowing position (Ruku)

In this position say:

Subhana rabbiyal azeem (3 times)
Glory be to my Lord who is the greatest

Next

Come up from the bowing position back to the standing position. As you are coming up say the following:

Sami-Allahu liman hamidah.
Verily Allah listens to one who praises Him

Now you should be in the standing position

In this position say:

Rabbana lakal hamd.
Oh our Lord, all praise is due to You

Next

Now go into the prostration (Sajdah) position. As you are going into this position say:

Allahu Akbar
God is Great

In the prostration (Sajdah) position you must ensure the following:

- The nose and forehead are touching the floor
- The two palms are on the floor with fingers together
- The two knees are on the floor
- The toes of both feet are erected and not laying flat on the floor

In this position say:

Sub-hana rabbiyal-a la. (3 times)
Oh God, glory be to You, the most High

Next

Now as you are coming up from the prostration position to the sitting (Jalsah) position say:

Allahu Akbar
God is Great

Now you are in the sitting (Jalsah) position; sit on the left thigh, with the left along the floor and the right foot upright. The toes of the right foot should be erected and the hands should be placed on the knees.

In this position say:

Rabbigh firlee war-hamnee (once only)
Oh Allah, forgive me and have mercy on me

Next

Go back to the prostration (Sajdah) position, while going back to that position say:

Allahu Akbar
God is Great

In the prostration (Sajdah) position say:

Sub-hana rabbiyal-a la. (3 times)
Oh God, glory be to You, the most High

Next

Now come up to the standing position stopping briefly in the sitting (Jalsah) position on the way.

As you are coming up say:

Allahu Akbar
God is Great

You have now completed the first unit (Rakat) of prayer

Performing the 2nd unit (Rakat) of prayer

Repeat all of the above steps from the 1st unit (Rakat), then instead of going to the standing position from the 2nd prostration (Sajdah) position return back to the sitting (Jalsah) position.

Now recite the following:

The Tashahud

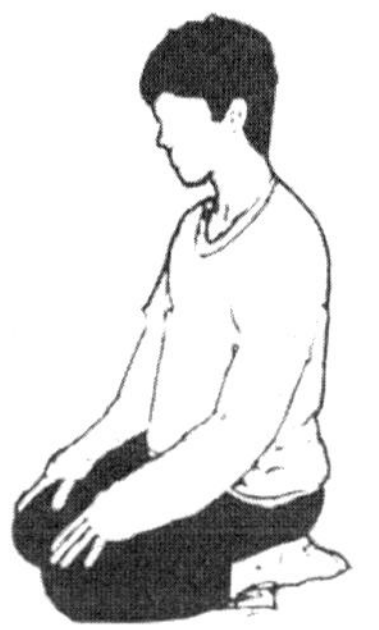

"At-tahiy-yatu lil-lahi was salawatu wat-tay yibatu.
Greetings, prayers and goodness belong to Allah

As-salamu 'alayka ay-yuhan-nabiy-yu
Peace be on you O Prophet

Wa rahma tullahi wa barakatuh
And the mercy of God and His blessings

As-salamu 'alayna wa 'ala 'ibadil-la his-saliheen."
Peace be upon us and the righteous slaves of God

"Ash hadu anla ilaha illal-llah
I bear witness that there is no god worthy of worship except God (While reciting this and the next part you should lift your index finger)

Wa ash hadu an-na Muhammadan 'ab-duhu wa rasuluh."
And I bear witness that Muhammad is His slave and Messenger

End of Tashahud

If you are praying a 2 unit (Rakat) prayer you should continue with the next stage which is the sending the peace and blessings (Darud) on the Prophet (peace be upon him) by saying:

"Allah humma sal-li 'ala Muhammad
O God, let Your mercy come upon Muhammad

Wa 'ala aa-li Muhammad
And upon the family of Muhammad

Kama sal-layta 'ala Ibraheem
As You sent prayers upon Abraham

Wa 'ala aa-li Ibraheem
And upon the family of Abraham

Innaka hameedum majeed."
Indeed, You are praiseworthy, Most glorious

"Allah humma barik 'ala Muhammad
Oh God, send your blessings upon Muhammad

Wa 'ala aa-li Muhammad
And upon the family of Muhammad

Kama barak-ta 'ala Ibraheem
As You sent blessings upon Abraham

Wa 'ala aa-li Ibraheem
And upon the family of Abraham

Innaka hameedum majeed."
Indeed, You are praiseworthy, Most glorious

Important

If you are performing the Maghrib prayer (sun set prayer) which has 3 units (Rakat) in total, stand and pray 1 more unit (Rakat) directly after you complete the Tashahud. Once you have completed the 3rd unit (Rakat), whilst in the sitting (Jalsah) position recite the Tashahud along with the Darud (sending peace and blessings upon Muhammad and Abraham - peace be upon them).

If you are performing the Zuhr (midday or noon), Asr (mid afternoon) and Isha (night) prayers which have 4 units (Rakats) in total, stand and pray 2 more units (Rakats) directly after you complete the Tashahud. Once you have completed the 4th unit (Rakat), whilst in the sitting (Jalsah) position recite the Tashahud along with the Darud (sending peace and blessings upon Muhammad and Abraham - peace be upon them).

If you are performing the Fajr (dawn) prayer which has 2 units (Rakats), you have nearly finished your prayer.

Upon completion of the Tashahud along with the Darud (sending peace and blessings upon Muhammad and Abraham - peace be upon them), finish the prayer with the Tasleem by doing the following:

Turn your head to the right and say:

As-salamu 'alaikum wa rahmatullah.
Peace and the mercy of Allah be on you.

Then turn your head to the left and repeat the same words:

As-salamu 'alaikum wa rahmatullah.
Peace and the mercy of Allah be on you.

The prayer is now complete.

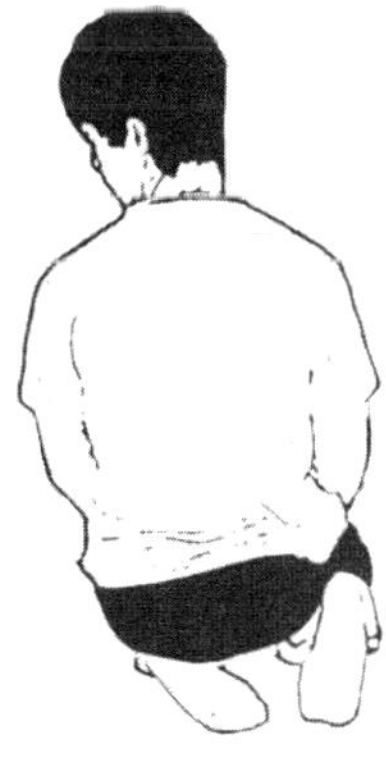

Short Qur'anic Chapters (Surah)

Any of the following chapters may be recited after Surat-ul Fatihah in the first two units (Rakats) of the prayer.

You are not limited to just these chapters. You should try and learn as many as you can (at your own pace and time).

Surah-al Asr (the time)

Bismillah hir-rahma nir-raheem.
In the name of God, the Most Beneficent, the Most Merciful

Wal asr.
By the time.

Innal insana lafil khusr.
indeed mankind is in loss.

Illalathina amanu wa aamilus-salihati watawas-subil
Haqqi watawas-subis sabr.
Except for those who have believed and done righteous deeds and advised each other to truth and advised each other to patience.

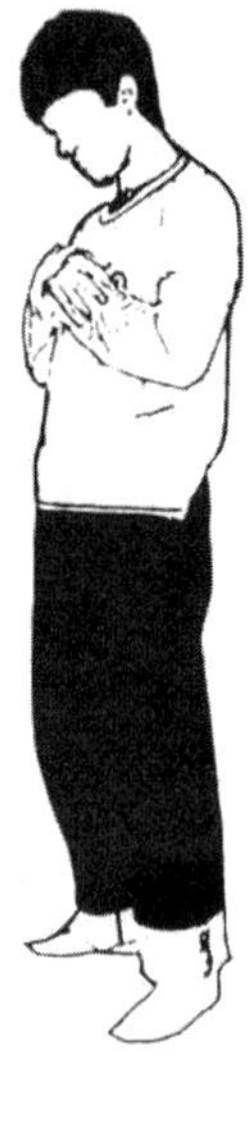

Surah-al Kawthar (the most abundant good)

Bismillah hir-rahma nir-raheem.
In the name of God, the Most Beneficent, the Most Merciful

Inna a-ataynaakil kawthar.
Indeed, We have granted you, (O Muhammad) Al Kawthar.

Fasali lirobbika wanhur.
So pray to your Lord and sacrifice (to Him alone).

Inna shaani-aka abtar.
Indeed, your enemy is the one cut off.

Surah-al Falaq (The daybreak)

Bismillah hir-rahma nir-raheem.
In the name of God, the Most Beneficent, the Most Merciful

Qul authu bi rab-bil falaq.
Say: I seek refuge in the Lord of the daybreak.

Min shar-rima khalaq.
From the evil of all that He has created.

Wa min shar-ri ghasiqin itha waqab.
And from the evil of the darkness of night when it falls.

Wa min shar-rin naf-fathati fil 'uqad.
And from the evil of those who blow into the knots (those who practice magic).

Wa min shar-ri hasidin itha hasad.
And from the evil of the envier when he envies.

Surah-al Nas (Mankind)

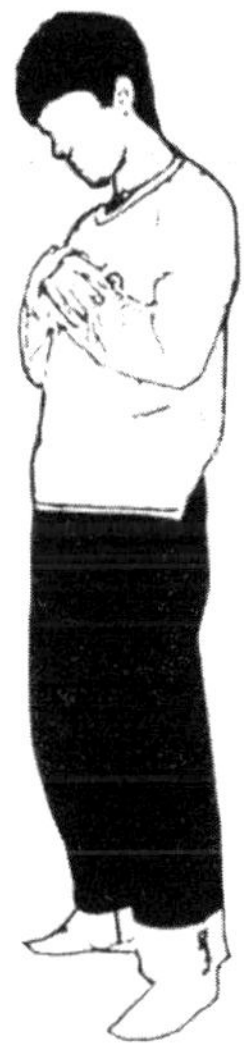

Bismillah hir-rahma nir-raheem.
In the name of God, the Most Beneficent, the Most Merciful

Qul authu bi rab-bin nas.
Say: I seek refuge in the Sustainer of mankind.

Malikin nas. Illa hin nas.
The Owner of mankind. The Lord of mankind.

Min shar-ril waswa sil khan-nas.
From the evil of the sneaking whisperer.

Allethi yuwaswisu fee sudu rin-nas.
Who whispers in the hearts of mankind.

Minal jin-nati wan-nas.
(whether he be) from among the jinn and mankind.

Spirit of Wudu[1]

The purpose of salat (prayers) is to purify a man of all evils. Ablution, or wudu, is the preparation of the body for this religious rite. Water is a great gift of God which is the best thing for washing all the impurities out of man. Similarly, salat is a 'divine spring' in which a man bathes and purifies himself of evil emotions and vicious thoughts.

Initiating the process of ablution (wudu) when a man puts water on his hands, he is, in effect, praying, 'O, God! Save these hands of mine from indulging in evil, and let whatever evil deeds I have indulged in through them be washed off.' Then he rinses his mouth and washes his face. At that time his soul prays silently, 'O, God! Kindly remove the bad effects of any improper food I have put in my mouth; the evil words I have uttered, and the evil things I have seen.' Thereafter, when he takes water in his hands and massages his head with his hands, his whole existence is moulded by the prayers, 'O, God! Wash away the bad effects of the evil ideas conceived by my mind and wrong plans devised by me, and cleanse and purify my mind.' When he washes his feet, this action of his becomes the entreaty before his Lord, that He may cleanse his feet of the dust of evil and make them (his feet) never tread any path except the path of righteousness and justice. In this way, the whole process of ablution assumes, so to say, the practical shape of the prayer, 'O, God! Make me a person who turns away from wrongs and one who keeps himself clear of evils.'

In normal circumstances, ablution is enough to create feelings of cleanliness in man, but the state of impurity (resulting from sex) is an extraordinary condition. So, in this state, washing of the whole body (ghusl) has been prescribed.

Spirit of Prayer[1]

Prayer, the second pillar of Islam, entails the worship of God five times a day in the prescribed manner. This mode of worship, laid down for mankind by God through His Prophet, is so all-embracing that one cannot imagine any superior way of worshipping the Almighty.

When the time for prayer comes, the greatness of God is proclaimed in the call to prayer, and the faithful are instructed to assemble for prayer as a matter of their own spiritual uplift. They then perform their ablutions—in so doing reviving their sense of cleanliness—and, fixing their minds on God, they make their way to the mosque, where they all offer prayers together. The prayers are led by an Imam, under whose guidance Muslims are shown how they should lead their lives. In the same way as the congregation make the Imam their leader in prayers, so should all Muslims unite around the Prophet, making him the focal point of their social existence.

The prayer has various stages: bowing low, prostrating oneself, and standing and kneeling before God. In assuming these various postures, the congregation demonstrate their submission to the Lord. When they stand, hands joined in prayer, when they bow low, when they sit reverently before the Lord, when they touch the ground with their foreheads, with each posture they adopt, they renew their covenant of submission to God.

During the prayers, an excerpt from the Quran is read out. One amazing attribute of the Quran is that, no matter which part is chosen and how much of it is recited, its message is clearly conveyed. This is because each page of the Quran is like a summary of the whole. In this way, any short excerpt from the

Quran recited in prayer suffices to show what pleases and what displeases the Almighty.

Besides this, the prayers include praise and remembrance of God, supplications to Him and the expression of goodwill towards the Prophet and all believers. The prayers then end with a message of peace to all mankind. Thus constituted, they are both an act of worship and a reminder of God's commandments. They give solace to believers, while creating social consciousness and unity in their ranks. Prayer is not only a symbol of the Islamic life, but also inculcates self-discipline among Muslims. Although the most important aspect of prayer is its being the main point of spiritual contact with God, it also has valuable lessons for us on how to conduct ourselves in our daily lives.

Prayer, as well as being a ritual mode of worship, is an expression of the inner realities of humility before, and devotion to God. The ultimate acknowledgement of another's greatness being the repetition of the words, "He is the Greatest," the words, *Allahu Akbar,* are uttered time and time again in prayer. Verbal acknowledgement is thus made of the absolute quality of God's greatness in comparison to that of ordinary mortals.

Physically, the ultimate recognition of another's greatness is the act of self-prostration; no physical act is more obviously a testament to the greatness of another than this. Performed repeatedly during prayers, it is a practical reminder and a clear demonstration of one's belief in the incomparable grandeur of God. The giving of one's entire attention to God is underlined by turning one's gaze towards the House of God. The direction in which one must face in order to pray is, therefore, of great religious significance, for it not only focuses one's attention on the deity, but also demonstrates that one's very life is turned towards God. Every aspect of one's life, from inner thoughts to outer needs, then becomes truly God-oriented.

When a servant of God bows before his Lord, and does so, not just as a matter of form, but in the spirit of true humility, the effect of his action does not remain confined to the domain, but extends to his everyday existence, pervading it completely. His thinking and actions bear the permanent stamp of his devotions, for it is impossible for a man to fear God and to bow before Him without being influenced thereby in his dealings with others. A true worshipper cannot be humble and meek before God and yet be arrogant and supercilious to his fellow men. He will not, of course, prostrate himself before them, nor will he address the words "You are great" to another person, as he would to God. But he will certainly avoid asserting his own superiority, and instead will adopt a humble demeanour on a parallel with his self-prostration before his Maker. The submission which he expresses in prayer to God becomes a reality in terms of his observance of others' rights. The very act effacing in the correct direction influences him to take a principled stand in his everyday dealings. At prayer in the mosque, he is the epitome of servitude to God: outside the mosque, he is the perfect character—humble in demeanour, morally upright, and kind, considerate and forgiving in all his transactions.

The important thing about prayer is that it induces the correct attitude in the devotee, as though the spirit of his prayers were keeping a watchful eye on everything he says and does. When going about his worldly affairs, it is as if the whole world were a mosque; his actions, therefore, at all times and in all places cannot be other than in consonance with what his worship requires of him.

1. Text taken from *Islam As It Is* by Sheikh Wahiduddin Khan, Goodword Books.

Eid Prayer

Eid prayer is a special prayer. It is offered on Eid-ul Adha and Eid-ul Fitr. It consists of two *Rakaat* (units) with six or thirteen additional *takbir*. It must be offered in congregation. The prayer is followed by the *Khutbah*.

There is no *Nafl* prayer before or after the Eid prayer. There is no *Iqamat* or *Adhan* for Eid prayer.

Two *Rakaat* of Eid prayer should be offered in the same manner as the 2 *Rakaat* of the usual prayer except that there are 7 *Takbir* in the first *Rakaat* and five *Takbir* in the second *Rakaat*. With each extra *Takbir*, the hands should be raised up to the shoulder level (As in *Takbir Tahrimah*).

All extra *Takbir* should be pronounced before starting recitation.

Funeral Prayer

It is a right of a Muslim that when he passes away, other Muslims should pray funeral prayer for him. It is supererogatory prayer. It should be prayed in congregation.

The *Imam* should stand level with the head and shoulders of the dead body if the body is male. *Imam* should stand level with the middle part of the body if it is a female.

Funeral prayer is only slightly different from other prayers in that there is no *Ruku*, no *Sajdah*, and no *Tashahud* in it. There is no fixed time for offering this prayer. It has to be prayed in a standing position only. Other conditions like purification, facing *Qiblah*, *Sutra*, dress etc. have to be satisfied as in the usual prayers.

Points to Remember

The aims of *salat* are:

- to bring people closer to Allah;
- to keep human beings from doing indecent, shameful and forbidden things;
- to purify the heart, develop the mind and comfort the soul;
- to remind people constantly of Allah and His greatness;
- to develop discipline and will-power;
- to guide people to the most upright way of life;
- to show equality, unity and brotherhood;
- to promote patience, courage, hope and confidence;
- to train people in cleanliness, purity and punctuality;
- to develop gratitude and humility;
- to show obedience and thankfulness to our Creator.

Voice of Islam Trust

Voice of Islam is a television show broadcast for the purpose of da'wah. It is produced by the Voice of Islam Trust, a non profit voluntary charitable organisation registered with the New Zealand government.

Voice of Islam delivers the message of Islam based on the teachings of the Noble Qur'an and the Sunnah (practices) of the Prophet Muhammad (peace be upon him). The show neither delivers nor promotes any political, national, ethnic, social or class perspective - its focus is purely on da'wah and deen al-Islam (the Islamic faith/way of life).

We need your support

Please support this noble project with your kind donation. Projects like Voice of Islam are of great importance for da'wah and solely depend upon your support and co-operation.

We urge you all to please support this humble programme by filling out the automatic payment form which can be downloaded from our website: www.voitv.org.

Or you can pay your donation directly into our bank account:

International Voice of Islam
Ecobank Ghana, Meridian Plaza Tema
Acc no. 0020094444366001
Swift Code: ECOCGHACTMA

May Allah (SWT) reward you?

Voice of Islam VOI TELEVISION

ANOTHER VOICE OF ISLAM COMMUNITY PROJECT

Bringing the message of Islam to all people

www.voitv.org